Selling On Amazon: How You Can Make A Full-Time Income Selling On Amazon

Reselling Products Found In YOUR Local Retail Stores with ZERO Risk & Unlimited Earning Potential

By Brian Patrick

Editor's Note:

This is the Step-by-Step Online Seller's Guide for anybody looking to make *full-time income in part time hours by selling on Amazon.* Specifically, this book will break down the proven process that I've used to sell consumer goods in the Amazon marketplace for high profit margins.

You WILL learn:
- How to identify profitable products that sell for as much as 5x the amount you pay for them
- Where and How to locate these golden items, how to get these products for even cheaper using savings techniques, and how to then resell these products for top dollar on Amazon
- How the FBA (Fulfillment by Amazon) program works and how to leverage it so Amazon is working for you
- Most importantly, you will learn how to become a profitable seller regardless of how much money you currently have

I've read a lot of material to fully understand the inner workings of this business, but there was not one resource that truly takes you from the starting line to the finish line. My goal was to fill this void, and after reading this book you will have no excuses as to why you aren't making just as much money as me or more within several week's time.

Requirements:

You do NOT need thousands of dollars, nor even hundreds of dollars to start. You do NOT need warehouse space. You do NOT need a business degree, e-commerce experience, NOR an extensive amount of free time. All that is required is Internet access, a few bucks, and a little hustle.

I have coined a term to describe this online selling business model because it differs from most online retail business. **Retail flipping** is the term I will refer to throughout this book when describing my processes. A typical online seller, Internet retailer, or third party seller will buy inventory from a wholesaler or distributor to then turn around and sell at a profitable markup. This is the most commonplace method for becoming an online seller.

The problem with this business model is that most people do not have the capital to purchase inventory in bulk and therefore cannot acquire items at a low enough price to sell for a profit. The barrier to entry is much too expensive, intimidating, and work intensive for any one individual to undertake.

For the majority of individuals looking to become an online seller, we will be discussing the methodology that anybody can follow; here is the synopsis of retail flipping:

Definition

Retail Flipping – \'rē ,tāl\'flip-iŋ\

1: Retail flipping is a term coined to describe a newly founded business model where profits are created by selling products online; the catch being that one acquires products to sell from brick and mortar retail stores.

2: Acquire inventory from retail stores; sell inventory in online marketplaces for profit.

...

Just like traditional and online retail, the retail flipping business model is founded on the long-standing principle of arbitrage. You may have heard the more common expression, "buy low, sell high". Using new technology and marketplaces, specifically Amazon, you can take advantage of this limitless opportunity.

For any given electronic product, you will find that it is priced differently across all stores, online marketplaces, and everywhere in between. The marketplace will never be perfect – e.g. a certain pair of headphones will never be for sale at the same price across all channels. This presents great opportunity to those willing to find products for sale at their lowest price point; they simply must know how to sell these products once they acquire them.

I not do buy my inventory from wholesaler distributors, nor do I buy from international exporters. The products that I sell are found in local shopping centers, hidden away in clearance sections, bought during major sales, and are even acquired from online marketplaces.

This book is my very own blueprint to acquiring product and selling it for more (sometimes for a 300-500% profit) utilizing Amazon as your marketplace. It describes the inner workings of my business and provides a guideline for any driven individual. Why would I disclose my business, you may be thinking?

In my journey to become an online selling expert, I've created this Book. I believe that by sharing my Retail Flipping model, more educated sellers will enter the marketplace. Competition is a good thing. New practices, ideas, methods, and technologies will help the selling community become more efficient. I was shown the ropes by a Pro Amazon Seller, and he's now doing better than ever, even with me now selling in the marketplace. We share ideas, collaborate on purchases, and help drive sales to each other's products.

Currently, online retail sales in the United States account for less than 20% of retail sales. Selling online, specifically selling on Amazon, is relatively new; there are new services and technologies made available everyday that make this business model even easier. While new techniques and technologies continue to pop up, the Retail Flipping method will continue to be a profitable, manageable venture for those looking to sell items online. Get ready to learn how you can become a profitable online seller in less than a month's time - It's time to retail flip!

Other Books By Brian Patrick

Selling On Ebay: The Beginner's Guide for How To Sell on Ebay

Disclosure:
The information contained in this guide is for informational purposes only.

I am not a lawyer or an accountant. Any legal or financial advice that I give is my opinion based on my own experience. You should always seek the advice of a professional before acting on something that I have published or recommended.

The material in this guide may include information, products or services by third parties. Third Party Materials comprise of the products and opinions expressed by their owners. As such, I do not assume responsibility or liability for any Third Party material or opinions.

No part of this publication shall be reproduced, transmitted, or sold in whole or in part in any form, without the prior written consent of the author. All trademarks and registered trademarks appearing in this guide are the property of their respective owners.

Users of this guide are advised to do their own due diligence when it comes to making business decisions and all information, products, services that have been provided should be independently verified by your own qualified professionals. By reading this Guide, you agree that my company and myself are not responsible for the success or failure of your business decisions relating to any information presented in this guide.

Table of Contents

Introduction: Why This Business Model is Profitable

This Book is meant to be a short, sweet, but totally encompassing look into my business model. I have included everything needed to start your own online selling business. If done correctly, you will be profitable within your first month of selling.

One of the best parts of this business is that there is very little barrier to entry. I have read and learned from other online resellers that started with just $50 and have achieved a full-time salary, all within their first year. Even better than that, I believe that you control how much you desire to earn. If you are looking for part time earnings, you can achieve it. If you are looking for full time earnings, you can achieve that as well.

To top it all off, this business is in its early stages. I learned about this business from a family friend. The first thing he asked me was, "What percentage of retail sales do you think is being done online in the U.S. today?" Has to be at least 50% of sales I thought, right? Wrong! Only 11% of all retail sales are being conducted online in the U.S. (this was a few years ago, but I remember vividly!). It has increased to closer to 15% and by 2014 it is projected to be a $250 billion dollar industry, with the majority of sales being computers, apparel, and consumer electronics.

Think back for a second...do you remember the Internet boom? What if you had been one of the first movers and shakers? Or if you had taken action during the real estate boom when housing prices quadrupled? There is no better time than now – and online sales are only going to increase drastically. This isn't a bubble that is going to burst, rather just the beginning of a new industry. Amazon has built a $50 billion dollar business around this concept, so I figured I would join the party and grab a slice of this exponentially booming pie. Now, let's get into exactly how you can get a slice of this pie and create the income you desire.

How I Got Started

I'm sure you were hesitant to purchase this book; I would have been doubtful too for such a claim as "make $2,700 a month in part-time hours". This isn't the most humble sales copy, but I wanted to grab you attention and I am also telling the truth. Plus, people love stories and love to read about other people's successes – So here is my story:

At the time of writing this, I am 24 years old. I live and work in New York City. I've always had an entrepreneurial spirit, but had placed it on the back burner during my college years as there were more pressing issues such as chasing girls and finding the next keg party. About midway through college, my best friend mentioned to me that his boss at his summer internship had begun selling items online. His boss was already the owner of a small business and was financially comfortable so I was curious as to why he would take on another venture.

That curiosity dissipated as summer came to a close and college was back in full swing.

Fast forward 3 years and my curiosity reignited. Also, student loans were kicking my ass and I was in the midst of a painstakingly long job search. With nothing to lose and college in the rearview mirror, my friend and I met with his former boss for a coffee and an informal introduction to selling on Amazon.

His boss told us that he was making an extremely high 6-figure salary by selling products on Amazon, all while still running and maintaining his original business that employed several people. A half hour meeting turned into a 2-hour crash course on what I now refer to as "retail flipping".

He didn't bother with the petty details such as making a seller account, or how to ship our products. He told us how he gets every single item he sells in the clearance section of his local Targets and Kohl's. He told us to look for items in stores that sell for 3x the price on Amazon. He broke down the industry as a whole and explained how e-commerce is on an exponential upswing.

He explained to us how Best Buy is "Amazon's Showroom" because people walk in to test the products and then use their smart phones to find a cheaper price on Amazon. He spoke to why so many brick and mortar retailers can no longer compete with online marketplaces. These brick and mortar retailers are not as efficient as new online retailers, and they end up having extra inventory and overstock products that need to be sold. To get rid of these products and make room for new inventory, prices are slashed. When this happens, there becomes an arbitrage opportunity and products can be acquired for 1/3 of the regular price. He also described how he uses Amazon's Fulfillment program (FBA), which handles all of his shipping and customer service needs (We will discuss the importance of this service later in the book).

On the way out of the coffee shop, our soon to be mentor looked down at his phone and chuckled to himself. I looked to my buddy to see if there was a joke I had missed, but he was clueless as well. We shrugged our shoulders and began to walk away. A few seconds later, we heard him shout, "20 of my products sold during our little chat, not a bad way to start the day eh?"

It wasn't more than a week later that my first shipment of products was on its way to the Amazon fulfillment center.

Fast forward to today, I still maintain a full-time job as New York City is one hell of an expensive place to live. However, I have crafted a retail-flipping model to my own liking and now put away several thousand dollars a month right into my savings account. We are going to walk through the step-by-step process that made this a reality for myself and in turn, you will learn to duplicate every step.

But before we get down to it, I want to summarize a recent month of sales. This real case study will hopefully provide some motivation, clarify the overarching process or retail-flipping, and help you better grasp the details of the later chapters

My Story: How I Consistently Earn $2,700 or More EVERY Month

Let's take an in depth look at what a now average month for me looks like. We will cover what products I acquire, how and where I acquire them, and then the breakdown of the various profit margins. This is a very accurate depiction of how I "Retail Flip".

I usually do not share such detail unless people are truly curious. Seeing how you've purchased this book, you deserve all the details – every last bit. This quick run through includes a lot of material that we will touch on later in this book, so do not get discouraged if not everything makes sense. We will break down this entire process, which I refer to as the Three Step Formula, in the following chapters.

Beginning of the Month - March

I sit down to go over my finances from the previous month to see how I performed. Using my custom-made excel workbook, I look at the month's totals to see that I profited around $2,800. My expenses were $5,900, this included the inventory, sales tax on the merchandise I bought, shipping charges from any online purchases, fulfillment supplies (boxes, tape), and shipping costs to get the inventory to Amazon warehouses. My net revenue was $8,700, which makes sense since $8,700-5,900 = $2,800 in profit. So by spending $5,900, I got back $8,700, which equates to a 47% return on my money. The top hedge funds have a hard time giving investors a 20% return on their investments.

The numbers look great, but I dig a little further to see how I could improve for the month ahead. The few months following the holidays are usually rough in terms of sales, so I stuck mostly to selling electronics and accessories that would accompany all those new gifts Santa left behind. I purchased a lot of toys at extreme discounts from the local Target, but wasn't surprised to see many of those didn't sell. This could have been avoided, but the deals were too good. Maybe I'll avoid the temptation next year, but the prices were low enough that they did not affect my sales. Because the holidays just ended, these toys will probably sit for quite some time, but will sell over the course of the year.

My best seller for the second month in a row was the Homedics Therapist Select SP-10H Shiatsu Pillow. I had found this product at an unbelievably low price online, which is usually very uncommon. Using my Kohl's charge card discount and an online coupon code, I was able to get these for approximately $16 each. I bought 200 of them. During this month of March, I was selling them for $69.99 and was selling about 3 a day. After Amazon's commission and the fulfillment costs, I was earning about $52 for every unit sold. The profit margin on these helped me reach my goals for several months since it was so high.

My Return = (52-16)/16 X 100 = 225% Return for a $38 Profit

Most products you buy and sell will not get this return, but you will learn how to spot these great deals and take advantage of them once you do find them. Had I only bought 10 of these, I would have had to work a lot harder during March to hit my profit goal. I was able to recognize the potential by analyzing the Amazon Sales Rank, the # of Reviews, and several other factors which we will get into in the coming chapters.

Let's Get Going this Month

After evaluating my past month's purchases, I made sure my checking account had received the appropriate bi-weekly payments from Amazon. The money was there; I was all set to go.

With all of my credit card payments documented in my excel document, I was able to see that all of the numbers made sense and no payments/credits were missing. With the funds in place, I paid off all of my credit cards in full. The remaining funds in my checking account was profit (the $2,800), and I deposited this into my savings account for safekeeping. My Amazon checking account was back to empty, but my credit card bill was paid and my savings got a nice boost.

With March in the books (literally), it was time to attack April. Working a full time position is limiting in several aspects when it comes to retail flipping. You miss a lot of sales that occur during the week, you can never be first to arrive at a store, and you don't have extra time to explore different stores and try new ideas. However, I like it this way. I work better knowing my time is limited, and avoid pitfalls many sellers hit. Having extra time just equates to more speculation. I have several friends that do this mostly full time and end up spending much more time than is needed. They will over think certain purchases, return items frequently, and just second-guess the system.

I have learned what works, what doesn't, and where the best returns can be found – all while working full time. Don't get discouraged if you only have a few hours a month to commit, you can be just as successful as full timers.

The New Month – April

My plan for April was to follow my normal routine. I mapped out when Kohls would be having their sales for the month. These sales enable charge card holders to receive up to 30% off products, and also receive an additional $10 in Kohl's Cash (gift card equivalent) for every $50 spent. I only shop at Kohls during these times, regardless of other sales and temptations. Aside from Kohls, I scheduled 4 times during the month when I make my rounds at the local Target, Bed Bath and Beyond, Toy's R Us, Marshalls, and occasional Radio Shack. In my area, there are about 3 shopping centers within a 25 mile radius that house all of these stores which I can hit in about 2-3 hours time depending on how good they're looking.

With these times entered into my calendar, I set myself up for success before the month even begins. Many retail flippers will sporadically scavenge their stores, but I rather miss a few deals here and there, than miss my scheduled visits. This ensures for long-term success, and allows me to pick times that won't affect my personal and professional life.

In addition to the Kohls' sales periods and weekly circuits, I chose one huge Book Sale to attend. I always go on the last day of the sale, usually this is Sunday. I do this because prices are usually slashed in half or books are given away for free/donation. This is a great way to get a ton of inventory for less than 100 or 50 bucks. I do not depend on this as an income source, but consistent visits help me accrue a large inventory and these boost sales in those tougher months. Usually, I will only buy books for $1 or less that will sell for close to $15 or more. After Amazon's steep commission fees for books, I will usually profit $7-9 per book. A lot of sellers make a full time living just doing books, but it requires a full time commitment and is hard to scale.

Lastly, I search for online deals throughout the month. I usually set aside 10 minutes a day to check several deal aggregator sites, bookmarked pages within major retailer sites like a Kohls or Best Buy, and Daily Deal sites like Woot.com.

We will get into more detail on all of these sourcing methods, but now you see how my monthly schedule looks. I try to make most of my purchases earlier in the month so I can get them into my inventory right away. In the long run this is not very important, but it helps me earn the majority of my profit in the same calendar month.

At Month's End

It's now the last few days of March and all purchases have been made. Here is what I was able to purchase:

Item	Store	Buying Price	Selling Price	~Profit
Skullcandy Hesh Headphones S6HEDZ-116	FYE	$40	$99	$45
Woodstock: 3 Days of Peace & Music Director's Cut (40th Anniversary Ultimate Collector's Edition and BD-Live)	Target.com	$30	$99	$55
NECA Bioshock 2 Exclusive Gift Pack Includes Subject Omega Figure,	Toys R Us	$30	$60	$23
Ultimate Direction Naviti Trail Waist Pack, Solid Blac	Marshalls	$16	$48	$24
Jensen JISS-20 Black iPod MP3 Dock Docking Speaker Station w/FM Radio	Kohls.com	$0/$5 for shipping(Paid with Kohls Cash)	$70	$58
Books (40)	Book Fair in Brooklyn	$35	$600 (40 books)	$400

These are not all of the products purchased, but they made up the majority of my expenses as I bought many units of each. Looking at these products, you can see that some achieve better profit margins than others. You also can see how the books add a nice layer of profit without shelling out a lot of capital.

Only a third of these books will sell within a few weeks, leaving many books for future sales. Selling books helps when starting out, as it requires very little capital and has the best margins by far. It requires more work and a more detailed approach, as you have to be careful in assessing the book's condition and assigning it an attractive price.

Closing the Books on April

I login to my seller's account on Amazon to check that my two payments were sent out for the month and crosscheck with my bank account. It was a slower month than usually, but I reached my $2,700 mark and a lot of items still have yet to sell. This will help me hit $3,000 in profit in the following months.

My obstacles for this month included a return to the store, over $1,000 in goods to the local Target, because of a sudden price drop. Their friendly 90-day return policy made this very smooth and there was very little headache involved. I did have a great surprise this month as well. I reached 10,000 frequent flier miles with my Capital One credit card, meaning I can now book up to $1,000 worth of flights for FREE.

Selling on Amazon: The BEST Online Marketplace to Sell and WHY

I have very little experience selling in other marketplaces, so I can't comment too much on their effectiveness. However, there are some clear distinctions and advantages that selling on Amazon provides. If you are new to online selling, it is good to understand all of the marketplaces so you can see firsthand how Amazon has changed the game.

There are several options in terms of marketplaces for online sellers to list inventory. The retail flipping model is successful across all marketplaces, but only Amazon creates such a lucrative opportunity and here's why:

The Brand

Ebay was once the big shot in the online selling game, but Amazon has since taken over. Don't get me wrong, Ebay is good for certain things such as selling hard to find items, vintage collections, and memorabilia. However, when it comes to brand image, Amazon instills the most confidence in buyers with their customer service based culture. Although both marketplaces allow third party sellers to list and sell their items, Amazon's emphasis on customer satisfaction to strengthen their brand has helped them become the premier online marketplace.

Premium Price

Backed by their superior brand, sellers on Amazon can expect to earn higher profits because customers are willing to pay more for the Amazon experience. I've even seen several professional sellers profit by purchasing items off Ebay and reselling on Amazon. You do not want to position yourself in a marketplace where you won't earn top dollar. This means that those Ebay sellers aren't achieving the full profit of their arbitrage.

Search Engine Optimized

While some buyers peruse the Internet, most people that intend to make a purchase know exactly what product they seek. They will Google the item they seek and go with the first listing that provides that product. Amazon realized the power behind being first in the search rankings, and have designed their website so these search engines favor their listings. Therefore, by selling your items on Amazon, you gain the most exposure possible. You will not have to spend one cent on marketing, ever.

*Recently, according to Forrester Research, Amazon has surpassed Google to become the number one starting point for online shoppers when looking for an item.

So not only will your product listings show up first in Google, but shoppers are now more apt to start their shopping search from within Amazon itself. No wonder their stock price has skyrocketed with current valuation in the $200 range.

Unlimited Growth Potential for your Business

"Their fulfillment service called Fulfillment by Amazon (FBA) is where the magic happens."

Fulfillment by Amazon is a new service offered by Amazon and has instantly become their competitive advantage as an online marketplace, and using FBA will become your competitive advantage over other third party sellers. FBA is an all-inclusive fulfillment service that works in unison with your Amazon seller account. You send them your entire inventory, they store and manage your inventory, and then they will ship your inventory to buyers when something is purchased, all on your behalf – all you have to do is send Amazon all of your products.

By utilizing this service, Amazon is now much more than just your online marketplace. They become your entire business – your warehouse, fulfillment house, customer service, and insurance plan. Let's go through a quick case study approach to what Amazon's FBA program can do for your business before we breakdown the specifics.

Hypothetical Example

You make your first sale! Amazon notifies you that customer "xyz" has placed the order and payment is confirmed. You box up your item, print off the shipping label, and take it to post office the following day. Congrats, you've made your first sale!

Six weeks later, you're selling 15 items a day on average. You have to box up, print shipping labels, and deliver all 15 items to the post office. Doable? Yes. But what happens when you hit 30 items a day, 50, 100? You become handcuffed by your own business.

There's not enough time in the day to do all this and you have to hire help. Or you decide to take it on yourself, but that leaves no one to hit the retail stores looking for new inventory. Not only that, but your dealing with returns now. You start receiving negative customer feedback because something was damaged. You're overworked and it's your own business!

Using Fulfillment by Amazon (FBA) eliminates most headaches that online sellers once faced, and allows them to focus on the important step in the three-step formula in the coming chapter, which is finding profitable inventory to sell.

The FBA Process

By opting in to FBA, you are making the conscious choice to allow Amazon to handle all of your orders, rather than yourself.

1. You send your entire inventory to one of Amazon's warehouses

where they will check each item in.
2. Once they've checked in your items, the items become available for sale on the Amazon marketplace.
3. Once an item sells, Amazon fulfills the order – they process the transaction, pick and pack the item, and ship out to your customer.
4. They also become your dedicated customer service center for any returns, refunds, and customer feedback.

This entire process is handled by Amazon, but managed by you when you sign into your seller account. You make all of the business decisions such as pricing your inventory, adding product descriptions, and important aspects that should be left to you. FBA will simply do all the grunt work, leaving you with time to monitor all the business decisions that ultimately affect your profit margin.

Benefits of FBA

We've touched on the basics of FBA and the important takeaways. There is a lot more behind to Amazon's Fulfillment program, but as long as you understand what it is and how it benefits your business, you're on your way to become a profitable seller on Amazon.

Let's quickly look at the two main benefits of enlisting in Amazon's FBA service.

Saves Time

Instead of shipping every item sold, you just send your entire inventory to Amazon in bulk. They will sort your items and mark them as ready for sale. You don't have to deal directly with customers. All returns, shipping offerings, promotional rebates, etc. is handled by Amazon and can be tweaked by you in the backend.

Increased Profits

When you free up your time, you can buy more products. When

you buy more products, you increase revenue. When you increase revenue, you increase profit.

How Much Does it Cost?

You are probably thinking that this FBA service must cost an arm and a leg. So did I, especially when my friend told us of all the headaches FBA has saved him. However, It's FREE to opt in to. That's right, FREE.

Once you have set up your seller account, you will have the option to enlist in this program. Any of the costs associated with FBA are variable costs, meaning you will only be charged for costs incurred once an item is sold. There are two costs that you will incur: monthly storage costs and fulfillment costs.

Storage costs: Currently it only costs $0.45/month per cubic sq. ft. to store your items with Amazon, with an increased rate of $0.60 during the holiday months.

Fulfillment costs: These costs vary for each product depending on the size, weight, and type of product and are charged to you only when a product is sold.

Both of these costs are standard costs for online sellers already, so you would be spending money for both of these services anyways. Amazon is such an efficient company that these costs are drastically low compared to other solutions or doing it oneself.

You should now understand why Amazon is the best choice for your online marketplace and the benefits of using their FBA service. We will go into further detail and instruction in leveraging all of Amazon's offerings when going through the Three Step Formula. In summary:

- Currently, Amazon is the best online marketplace for third party

sellers
- Branding, Premium Pricing, and Search Engine Optimization continues to make Amazon the #1 online retail destination, all of which you can leverage.
- Amazon's FBA service is the competitive advantage you will need to build a powerful, efficient business.

Now you are prepped to become an Amazon third party seller. With Amazon as your online marketplace and the fulfillment services at your disposal, you are ready to learn the Three Step Formula to becoming a profitable Retail Flipper.

The Three-Step Formula

The entire selling process I follow can be categorized into THREE steps. Each step involves its own processes, resources, and time management. Some steps are more involved than others, but here are the three steps we will cover:

1. Finding Best Selling Inventory with a Profitable Markup
2. Leveraging the Amazon Marketplace to Sell Your Items
3. Just Rinse and Repeat – Fueling Your Selling Machine

These steps cover all of the critical aspects of selling on Amazon. We won't cover non-revenue generating tasks such as navigating the Amazon Seller dashboard or contacting Amazon Customer Service. Any of this information is readily available on the Amazon Seller's Website. There is no reason for this book to repurpose their content when you can simply find any answer in their documentation.

Anyone capable of capitalizing on this retail flipping business model is more than capable of handling the minute, administrative responsibilities of maintaining a seller's account. Of course, we will cover all such tasks that impact sales, revenue, and the success of your online selling venture.

Finding Best Selling Inventory with a Profitable Markup

The most difficult, but critical aspect of the retail-flipping model is: Step 1 – Finding Best Selling Inventory with a Profitable Markup.

However, this is the step that I enjoy the most, and have perfected to the best of my ability. This is where "Retail Flipping" gets is name. Unlike most other online sellers, retail flippers find inventory to sell in other retail stores. I am not getting my products from a wholesaler, a Chinese manufacturer, or my buddy's sketchy uncle down in Panama. My products come from the exact retail chains you have in your town and in every town across the U.S. I am talking about your Home Depots, Walmarts, Targets, Macy's, etc…

Since the beginning of the marketplace (probably the stone age), one simple principle has been its driving force. That principle is arbitrage. It is the simple act of buying a product in one market and selling it in another for a higher price. We all can recall a time where we've purchased a product only to find that it was $20 cheaper at another store. Without the driving force of arbitrage, merchants would not be able to make a profit and therefore the marketplace would not exist.

You may be thinking that the Internet has destroyed arbitrage because everybody can see all of the prices of a product across all marketplaces. This is true…somewhat. You may be able to see that a certain pair of headphones is 5 dollars cheaper on Buy.com versus Walmart.com. Or that Amazon is charging more for a pair of sunglasses you found on the manufacturer's website.

But…would you know that the Ipad 2 case you just purchased online was 30 dollars cheaper in their brick and mortar store? Yes, if you went to that store. Yes, if you knew the exact store. Yes, if you had the time to sit in traffic on your way to the store. Yes, if the item was in stock that day. Yes, if you had the coupon to reduce the price. Yes, if you were registered for the super savings card.

So…Yes, the information that a particular Ipad 2 case is $30 cheaper in store is available. But what percentage of the American population knows this? And if so, what percentage prefers spending their limited free time waiting in traffic, dealing with crowds, just to save $30?

A very, very small percentage (I am one of the few and you can be too). Not only that, many of these consumers that end up paying a premium online, knowingly choose to do so. Whether they don't have the time, whether it's their kid's soccer practice, whether they live where there is no store, whether their time is more valuable than $30, there's a reason.

Sorry I got carried away there, but this is why arbitrage still exists in today's marketplaces; this is why retail flipping will continue to thrive. The price difference between a product found in a brick and mortar store and an online marketplace is where profits are made. This is the foundation of retail flipping. Without this differential, you would not be reading how I earn close to 3k a month in revenue.

Got It! So What Exactly do I buy?

Once people understand how I operate, the next question that always follows is: What do you buy? Simply put: I buy everything - electronics, consumer goods, seasonal products, books, CDs, video games, mostly anything with a big enough arbitrage opportunity.

I do stay away from certain types of products such as apparel and jewelry to name a few. Just using common sense you can determine what product categories will succeed. For example, clothing is not the best category as there are different sizes, colors, and variations of the same shirt. This makes listing products online a lot harder. Also, a clothing product is more likely to get returned if it doesn't fit right or is in the incorrect size.

My favorite categories include toys, electronics, and personal care products. However, my mentor who introduced me to this business model operates in entirely different categories. There are endless amounts of products out there, and you will find certain niches that you are more comfortable in. You will quickly find that mostly anything that sells in stores, also sells online so don't stress this question.

Found Something! How do I know if I should buy it?

This is probably the most asked question, and it should be. As stated earlier, in order for you to make a profit, there has to be a difference between the purchase price of an item and the price for which it will sell. Keeping it simple, I tend to look for items that are generally at least a 2.5x markup. This means that I will only buy a $10 product if it will sell for $25 online. The markup has be at least this high because certain costs come into play, which we will get into later.

However, there are exceptions. Sometimes I may buy a product with only a 2x markup if I know that it's a hot selling item that will sell quickly. For example, I recently purchased an iPad accessory at a price of $15 that was only selling for $30 (2x markup) because I knew it would sell very quickly. Once you get the hang of it, you will be able to identify products that will sell almost instantly and therefore pose almost no risk.

In this instance, my profit margin is not as high, but I am able to quickly sell the product and the funds will appear in my next bi-weekly payment from Amazon. Since I like to pay my credit cards in full every month, these hot selling products are ideal. I am able to purchase these products with my credit card, and will receive payment within the same billing cycle – making my finances very easy to manage.

On the contrary, you may come across products with a 5x-10x markup that aren't hot selling products. Examples of such products include toys on clearance after the holiday season. Prices are slashed, and you get toys for up to 95% off. However, these toys will most likely not sell until summer time or even the next holiday season depending on how popular the toy is. If you have the funds, you can acquire a massive amount of inventory for next year's holidays during the post-holiday months. Don't expect to sell a lot of these products right away, but your margins will be amazing and you will make a killing during next year's holiday season.

Know Your Marketplace

In the previous chapter you discovered that the Amazon marketplace is the best choice for your online selling business. By understanding your marketplace, you can dissect what products are best for selling on Amazon. There are certain metrics that Amazon uses to organize products, all of which are vital for Amazon Sellers to understand. This information is readily available on Amazon's product listings. Learn how to breakdown the following information and your life as an Amazon Seller will become drastically easier.

There are four components of a product listing that you should focus on: Price, Amazon Sales Ranking, Feedback, and Competition. All of these factors are readily available on each product's listing on Amazon. You can visit Amazon.com if at home or use a simple smartphone app to help you research these factors when out in the stores. We will discuss the tools of the trade later, but for now you must understand what to look for.

The Four Factors to Identifying Winning Inventory

In this exact order, these 4 factors should always be analyzed before making a purchase:

Price

Simply look at the price of an item. If I can't achieve my 2.5x markup, I'll usually stay away from a product. On the flipside, if there is a 5x markup on an item, this may help me decide to buy more of that item. Always check price first, because if there isn't a profitable margin then there's no need to move forward. Some months are better than others and this will also influence my decision on pricing. If there aren't many deals to be found I may buy a deal with a markup of only 1.5x.

If you want to fully calculate how much profit a certain product will generate, you can use the FBA calculator. You can input the proposed product into the calculator as well as the current price for which it is selling, and the calculator will determine how much money you will receive from each sale. It will deduct the commission Amazon takes, as well as the certain fulfillment costs associated with that product such as shipping and packing, and return the final dollar amount you will receive from each sale. You can find the link to this calculator at the end of the book in the resources section.

Example:

I recently purchased some tablet computers for $80 that were only selling for $120. Even though the markup was only 1.5x, I was able to profit $25 on each tablet because the price point was high enough and I knew they would be hot sellers based on the other criteria we will get in to.

Exceptions:

Never buy items that sell for less than $10-15 (except books) even if there is a high markup. After Amazon commission fees, you will be looking at a single digit profit number and you will have to sell a large quantity of those items. This is an inefficient use of your time and resources for such a low payout.

That doesn't mean avoid buying low priced items, just be sure that they are selling for higher than $15.

One of my best purchases to date was an assortment of decorative stocking holders at Target. They were only $2 after heavy markdowns since the holiday season was over. I could have looked past these items, but was happily surprised when I saw they were selling for $25 on Amazon. I bought all 20 remaining items for a whopping total of $40 and profited close to $400.

Amazon Sales Ranking

So you've found a product that meets your pricing standards and now want to check the Amazon Sales Rank. The Amazon Sellers Ranking is a numerical valuation assigned to each product based on the quantity sold everyday on Amazon. This ranking is specific to Amazon only, and ultimately is a comparison metric across all of the products available for sale on Amazon. Since you can't directly tell how many units of an item are being sold everyday, this is a great alternative for determining how popular an item is.

How it works - based on actual sales and updated hourly, Amazon assigns a relative number to each product. The lower the number is, the more popular the item is which equates to higher sales. For example, if one pair of headphones has an Amazon ranking of #300 and an anti-snoring pillow has a ranking of #1,200 – you can determine that more headphones are being sold than the anti-snoring pillow.

In addition to a product's overall Amazon Sales Rank, there usually is a categorical sales rank attributed to each product. Amazon will provide an overall Sales Ranking or Categorical Ranking, usually never both. For example, the anti-snoring pillow mentioned above may have an overall Amazon Sales Rank of #1,200, but it may have a Sales Rank of #35 within the Personal Care category. This would indicate that it is the 35th most sold personal care product on Amazon, and only 34 personal care products sell more units everyday.

Example:

You identify a product you want to purchase. It has a great price markup and you know want to check the Amazon Sales Ranking. You find the product listing on Amazon and scroll down to the description area to find that the product, the Homedics Sp-20h, has an Amazon Sellers Rank of #3,812 in the Health and Personal Care Category.

This means that there are 3,811 Health and Personal Care products selling more quickly at this point in time. Unless you know how many total items there are in the Health and Personal Care category, this ranking may seem useless. Amazon does not publish or disclose the amount of products in each category.

To make sense of this ranking, you must familiarize yourself with the various categories. This is just something you will learn by getting use to the different categories and how your items sell. Once you find your niche(s) of product types, you will easily internalize a familiarity with the rankings and the Amazon Sales Rank will become your best friend.

I actually had the item mentioned above, the Homedics Sp-10h, and sold several units everyday. I had little experience in this category, but after testing the waters I now know that items in this category with a sales rank of 5,000 will sell very fast. I can then infer that items with a ranking of under 10,000 in this category will probably be good purchases and will most likely sell with ease.

Exceptions:

When doing your research on potential products to buy, you may come across product listings that do not offer an Amazon Sales Ranking. While rare, this will occur for various reasons. Usually it's just an error with the product listing, or improper categorization, and should not discourage you from selling such product. You will just have to weigh the other 3 factors more heavily in your decision process.

Customer Feedback

Once Price and Sales Ranking has been analyzed, you will look to customer feedback or customer reviews. When looking at feedback, I am looking at <u>three</u> things: the total rating out of 5 stars, the number of reviews, and when the most recent feedback was left.

The total rating will simply tell you if that product is one of quality. Most people are extremely critical these days, so anything above 3 stars if perfectly fine. I've sold items with 2 star ratings and had no problems. I usually stay above 3 stars when purchasing items. By looking at this factor you will quickly learn which brands are reputable and which brands to avoid. After the first month of retail flipping, I was able to easily pickup any consumer electronic good and determine the quality just by seeing who made it. You will quickly understand your niche(s) and which brands produce the most popular, quality products.

The number of reviews is much more important because this will tell you several things. First, reviews of any kind show that purchases have been made. Second, the more reviews an item has, the more items have sold. Many times you will come across products with no reviews and you should avoid these items if possible. Although they could turn out to be good sellers, there are enough deals on proven products to avoid the risk.

It's also important to note that some products just happen to receive less feedback. This can be because the item does a fairly simple task and does not need much feedback such as a pencil sharpener or a jump rope. Those items either work or they don't, and will simply get returned if they don't work. Also, really high quality item sometimes don't get as much feedback because they work flawlessly and customers have nothing bad to say.

The last and most overlooked aspect of feedback is the date of when feedback was given. I check the most recent date of feedback to ensure it has been purchased recently. I do this because sometimes products become outdated and older models stop selling (this happens a lot in technology based categories). I've purchased several items that had over 100 reviews, but none of which were recent. I had to return these items because I failed to fully analyze all components of customer feedback.

Competition

Lastly, I'll see how many sellers have this product for sale. Competition can be good; it usually means that the item sells really well and there is room for many sellers to profit. It can be bad as well. Rookie sellers will compete strictly on price and not on profit, driving the sales price to spiral downward. Also, every seller will have a minimal profit point for which they need to sustain business.

For example, you may be looking to earn a $15 profit on an item, but your competition may only need to make $2 for them to sustain business. Also, you'll never know the price for which acquired the product for.

Alongside you and the other third party sellers, you will sometimes compete against Amazon. Amazon will acquire and sell many products directly. If you can offer a better price than Amazon, than have no worries because your listing will come up as the best price. However, understand that Amazon, just like other sellers, can lower their price to reclaim the best offer. Competing with Amazon is a little scarier than other sellers because they can always beat you on price although they usually maintain market prices.

Don't be scared of competition because it will always be there. It has yet stopped me from making money; it helps me identify the best products to acquire.

How can you analyze all these factors while looking for products?

Amazon has created a smartphone App – "Amazon Price Checker" just for you...well not really. They've created this app to arm their customers with a mobile, cost savings tool. Savvy consumers will go into brick and mortar retail stores (just like us!) and use this app to scan barcodes of items they are interested in. The app will bring up the product listing on Amazon, and consumers can determine if they can get a better price purchasing from Amazon.

My online selling business relies heavily on this app. Instead of identifying products that are cheaper on Amazon, I use this app to find products in stores that are cheaper than those listed on Amazon. When you scan an item's barcode/UPC guess what comes up? The Price, Amazon Best Seller's Rank, Customer Feedback, and Competition. As long as your phone is charged and receiving service, you can analyze the 4 Factors of winning inventory on the go.

You've made it through Step One. You've successfully found hot selling items with a great markup of 2.5x. Although these products can be found everywhere, I've created a wide range of resources to help guide you as to where and how to buy your products in the most effective and cost saving ways. This section is called "The Ultimate Resource Section for Finding Profitable Inventory" and is found at the end of the Book. With the hardest step out of the way, lets move on to Step Two.

Leveraging the Amazon Marketplace to Sell Your Items

The hard part is over, and therefore the profit has already been made. While there are still remains several variables that affect the profitability of your inventory, your hard work will mostly get rewarded.

"Your profit is determined when you buy your inventory, not when you sell it."

While you don't have full control of how much your items will sell for, you can control how much those products cost to acquire. If you are diligent in your search for highly profitable items in Step 1, no remaining factors will have much impact on your inventory selling. Some competition and pricing changes will come into play, but your 2-3x margin will provide more than enough room to handle any miniscule price drop.

It's similar to Warren Buffet's famous expression for investing:

"You leave yourself an enormous margin of safety. You build a bridge that 30,000-pound trucks can go across and then you drive 10,000-pound trucks across it. That is the way I like to go across bridges."

With your highly profitable items ready to go, all that remains is sending your items into Amazon and leveraging their FBA services to reduce the amount of work you will need to do.

I've broken down this process into several steps for organization purpose. However, all of the steps should take very little time once you get the hang of it. The hardest aspect of retail flipping, finding profitable product, is in the rearview – this step simply requires patience and attention to detail.

Getting Started

Instead of reiterating the steps to opening a Seller's Account on Amazon, we will defer to Amazon to clearly state how to get started. I would suggest that you visit Amazon's Seller Central (http://services.amazon.com/content/sell-on-amazon.htm) to read up on any questions you may have. There are a few important things I'd like to address just to save you some time and clarify any thoughts you may have right now.

- You do not need to own a business or an LLC to sell on Amazon. As an individual seller, you can simply supply a bank account for payment purposes and your SSN for tax purposes.

- There are two types of payment structures for operating an Amazon Seller Account. You can pay a monthly fee, currently $39.99 a month plus any associated fees (Amazon's commission), or you can pay a $0.99 fee plus any associated fees (Amazon's commission) for every product sold. Simply put, start with the $0.99 per sale fee structure. When you begin selling more than 40 products a month, switch to the monthly $39.99 fee as it will be more cost effective.

- As previously mentioned, you will also need to enlist for the Fulfillment by Amazon service. Although optional, we've already explored how leveraging FBA is one of the key components to your success when selling on Amazon. It's a simple service that you enroll in once you've opened your Seller Account.

Ninety percent of your time will be spent back in Step One as you hunt for deals. The remaining ten percent will fall into the following process. With your Seller's account in place, and FBA services enlisted, let's get started.

*Again, you must sign up for your Amazon Seller's Account

(http://services.amazon.com/content/sell-on-amazon.htm) and enlist in the Fulfillment by Amazon (http://services.amazon.com/content/fulfillment-by-amazon.htm) program before moving forward.

Uploading Product

In the top left navigation, you will select "Add a Product". This is where you will enter the Barcode/UPC of your item (the number you've scanned with your Price Checker App). Several matching listings will pop up and you will have to go through and choose the appropriate listing. Usually your product will appear right away, but sometimes you may have to weed through incorrect listings and similar products.

The right listing will be the one that has the most reviews, contains all of the product information, and ultimately is the listing that you judged your purchase off of. Other sellers will get sneaky and try to create additional listings for the same product, but this is stupid for 2 reasons. A) Amazon will catch you and suspend your seller's account. B) Anybody searching for your product will be directed by the Search Engines to the listing with the most reviews and proper description.

*You do have the option of creating a listing for a new product that has yet to have been listed on Amazon. My retail flipping method does not include this strategy because you have little indication as to see if your item will sell ahead of time. I know people that successfully make their own listings, but it creates more work and is much riskier by nature.

Completing the Listing

After choosing the correct listing, you will have to enter certain information, such as if the product is new or used. All of your products will be new, unless you decide to sell used books as discussed earlier in which case you will assign a certain condition of used (like new, good, etc.).

Assigning the Price

Amazon helps you determine the price as it suggests you match the lowest price at that time. Although helpful, you should always look at the item's listing one more time. You will find that the lowest price suggested by Amazon is usually correct, but you may want to consider pricing differently because you are an FBA seller and here's why:

FBA sellers not only leverage the fulfillment operations of Amazon such as the storage, packing, and shipping, but by using FBA, sellers are able to sell their items at a premium price. The three benefits are listed below:

- FBA listings garner more attraction because they are marked with a Fulfillment by Amazon notice – this is a huge trust factor for buyers. Buyers will rather purchase from a third party seller using Amazon's fulfillment services, than a third party seller who will do the shipping and handle returns themselves.

- FBA items are eligible for free Super Saver Shipping and Prime shipping. This means buyers will be enticed to purchase from you over other Non-FBA sellers because Amazon will offer free shipping to them. (Since Amazon is making some money from you using their fulfillment services, they prefer that buyers purchase from FBA sellers.)

- FBA items qualify for customer service direct from Amazon, just like any products purchased directly from Amazon. This further increases buyer trust as they know they can return their items to a huge company, rather than a mom and pop shop that may provide hazy return policies.

The product you are listing will have several sellers, all of whom can be sorted on the product's listing page. You can sort all of the sellers of your item by those using FBA, and those doing the fulfillment themselves. From here, you will be able to determine the lowest price offered by a FBA enlisted seller and can match that price accordingly. Everyone's pricing strategy will be different.

I like to match the lowest FBA price in an effort to achieve quick turnover with my products, allowing me to pay my credit cards in full and start fresh every month. Other sellers, with more capital, will wait me out in an attempt to achieve better margins. It all depends on how much capital you are willing to pump through the retail flipping business model.

Sale Price

Amazon allows you to create a Sale's Price for your listing. For marketing purposes, I always utilize the sale pricing option. Amazon gives you the option of setting a sale's price in which you can offer a price that is lower than the regular asking price, for a certain number of days.

I will set the regular price at $10-20 higher than I would like to receive, and then set my Sale's price at the actually price I want it listed for. I will make the sale last several months just so this pricing structure remains. All you are doing here is adding another layer of marketing and increasing the conversion rate of your customers. They will get the impression that they are getting the item on sale, as they will see a regular price crossed out and a sale price highlighted. If you peruse through various Amazon product listings, you will see that this method is often used.

Inventory and Shipments

With the items uploaded into your inventory and pricing defined, you are almost ready to ship. To clarify, since you using Amazon's FBA service, you are not shipping products to customers – you are shipping all of your products to Amazon, for they will be doing the packaging and shipping on your behalf. If you are still a little unclear about Fulfillment by Amazon, please visit the FBA Website. (http://services.amazon.com/content/fulfillment-by-amazon.htm)

Inventory Types

Before you initiate your first shipment, Amazon mandates that you select one of two inventory processes. The two options for sending your inventory into the Amazon Fulfillment center are 1) Stickered Inventory & 2) Stickerless, Commingled Inventory.

Stickered Inventory

By selecting Stickered Inventory, you will have to label every single item in your shipments before sending to Amazon. This is somewhat easy to do by yourself, as Amazon prepares the labels into one document to print out. If you have a label printer, this process is not too daunting. The benefit of labeling your items is that you're ensuring that when somebody purchases your product, they actually receive your product.

Stickerless Inventory

By selecting Stickerless, Commingled Inventory, your products do not need to be individually labeled. Your products will not receive an individual label, and they will be placed with identical items upon arrival at Amazon's fulfillment center. When somebody purchases your item, any one of the available products (regardless if it is yours or another seller' product) can be used to fulfill the order. The benefit of commingled inventory is that you do not have to spend time or money labeling your products.

Exception: All items that are categorized, "Media Items", must be labeled. These items, such as DVDs, CDs, and books, must be labeled because every item has a different condition. You would not want somebody to buy your DVD, but then receive a bootleg DVD from another seller because your items were commingled.

I am an advocate of Stickerless, Commingled inventory because most of my items are generic games, electronic goods, or personal care products. It makes no difference to me whether my buyer receives my actual electric razor or another seller's. It saves me time and Amazon's customer service team can handle any problems that could further arise.

If you decide to go with Stickered Inventory, I would suggest paying Amazon to the labeling for you. They currently offer this service now for $0.20 an item. This will cut into your margins, but save you plenty of time in the long run. They will label your items for you upon arrival at their fulfillment center.

Create Shipment

With your inventory type selected, you can now create and send out your first shipment. Let's say you want to send in 10 headphones. You've found the correct listing and submitted a quantity of 10 at a sale price that matches the lowest FBA price. You've hit the "Save and Finish" button, which confirms this item as added.

Packaging Options

You are now at the next screen, where you have the option of sending them in as individual items or case packed items.

Individual Items

By selecting individual items, you are telling Amazon that you will be adding different items to this shipment.

Case Packed Items

By selecting case packed items, you are telling Amazon that you have a larger quantity of this same product and will be only sending this product in this shipment.

Unless you have a large quantity of a single item, always select "individual items". This will allow you to add other items to your shipment, which will help lower the cost of the shipment since you can place everything in the same box. You will then move to the next screen where Amazon will assort your inventory into different shipments.

Sometimes Amazon will split up your items in different shipments. They do this because their different fulfillment centers may be short on an item and will need to restock in order to fulfill customer orders closer to the geographic location of that fulfillment center. There is not much you can do about this. You may end up having to send 3 separate boxes to 3 different fulfillment centers, increasing your cost of shipping products to Amazon.

To help minimize these cots, I suggest that you wait until you have a large amount of products to ship out. You will end up filling up large boxes, and this helps reduce the cost. Also, this process is much easier when you do product uploading and shipping tasks together, rather than trying to do it every few days.

Adding More Items To Your Shipment

Once you've listed your first item and have placed it into a shipment, you are prompted to either continue working on that shipment, or return to it later. If you have more items to sell, you will just repeat the earlier instructions for listing your products.

After you've listed another item, you will most likely have the option to add that item to the existing shipment you started, rather than creating a new one. This is a good thing, so select "add to existing shipment" and now this shipment will begin to contain several of your products.

If there is no option to add to an existing shipment, you will have to create a new shipment. Again, Amazon does this based on their inventory needs and there is little you can do to avoid these multiple shipments.

Also, Amazon will sometimes have you place a few of the same items in different shipments. For example, you may have 10 pairs of headphones to ship out. After you've listed the products, and have chosen the "individual items" packaging option, Amazon will prompt you to send 6 headphones in a shipment to the Arizona Fulfillment Center, and then add the other 4 headphones to a shipment going to Massachusetts. This is normal, and you just need to follow their instructions.

I always have my inventory piled away in one corner of my room, and then have several boxes opened up across the room. After every product listing, I follow Amazon's prompted instructions and place the correct amount of the items with their corresponding shipments. This may sound confusing, but Amazon's shipment cue screen makes it really easy to match up your inventory with what boxes they should be in.

Working on Shipments

Once you have listed all of your products and have placed them in appropriate groupings (either in the boxes like me or a different way), you will be ready to prepare the shipments.

In the first section, you will make sure the quantity set is correct. Quickly make sure that your providing the exact quantity of inventory assigned to the shipment in progress.

The next section, Label Items, will only occur if you have selected Stickered inventory OR the inventory you are sending are Media

Items. Amazon will prompt you to print out the labels and will suggest the type of label paper you could use for printing. With these labels printed out, you will now affix them to the appropriate inventory. Amazon mandates that you place these labels over the UPC label found on your item.

As mentioned earlier, I prefer the stickerless inventory option so I can avoid this step. However, if I am selling any used books that month, I have no choice but to affix labels to the books.

The third section, Select Carrier, is where you will choose your shipping method. Like most retail flippers, you will be selecting "Small Parcel Delivery" which simply means you will be sending in individual boxes and NOT pallets or shipments over 150lbs. In the next section, you will choose the Amazon-Partnered Carrier option. Amazon has partnered with UPS to give its FBA sellers greatly discounted shipping costs. There is no reason in the world not to select this option and have UPS be your carrier. These rates are very cheap, helping you reduce your shipping costs.

The next section, Prepare Shipment, will simply ask you for the number of packing slips you will need. Here is where you will begin to actual package your items. If you can fit all 10 of those headphones in one box (you better!), then all you will need is 1 packing slip. Each box needs its own packing slip, so just enter the number of however many boxes you needed to pack up all of your items in that shipment.

To clarify, one shipment may contain more than 1 box. The term shipment just dictates that all of the products in that shipment be sent to the same Fulfillment Center. Shipments may contain 100's of products, in which case you will need several boxes (each containing a packaging slip) to complete the shipment.

After printing out your packing slip(s), you will head to the next section, Provide Details. Here you will enter the dimensions of your box as to determine the shipping cost. After providing details, Amazon will give you a shipping cost based on their discounted rate and your shipment's dimensions.

Once you give the consent, Amazon will provide the UPS labels for you to print and affix to the outside of your box. Make sure you have already labeled each item, if needed, and have placed the packing slip on top of your items before taping up the box and attaching the shipping label.

*Tip: Make a UPS account online and you can order shipping labels, 50 at a time, for FREE. They will deliver these labels right to your door the very next day. They do this because they want you shipping with them. These labels would otherwise cost you $15 a package at Staples or anywhere else.

*Tip: Buy boxes in bulk from your nearest Home Depot. I usually purchase the Large boxes as it provides the most cost effective dimensions when using UPS as your partnered carrier.

Completed Shipment

You've done it! Your first FBA shipment is completed. The shipping cost will be deducted from your Seller Account's balance or charged to your credit card on file if a sale has yet been made. You can schedule a UPS pickup to your residence for a small fee or drop off your boxes to your local UPS shipping office.

Amazon will receive your shipment in a few days, check to make sure the inventory claimed is actually there, and then mark your inventory as available for sale. When logged in to your seller account, you will see all of your products that are available for sale. Under the inventory menu item, select manage inventory. This will provide you the entire list of your products, the remaining quantity, and allow you to make changes to the price and other product listing details.

What's Next

Depending on the prices you've set for your inventory, and several other factors, Amazon will determine where your offer ranks on the product listing. The best offering is placed in the "buy box". This is extremely powerful position. If the buyer isn't aware of all the other sellers' prices and simply hits add to cart, the seller in the buy box makes the sale.

Many people aren't aware that Amazon is like Ebay and allows third party merchants to sell on their platform. Most of my friends and family assumed they are buying directly from Amazon, and weren't aware that most products are being provided by third party sellers. They assumed that there is one price for such item, and will add to cart without looking any further.

About two-thirds of my products reach the "buy box" position. This is a combination of my ability to find great inventory and offer the lowest the price, and the preferential treatment offered by Amazon since I am an FBA seller.

If you and three other sellers all have the same asking price, you will be the "box seller" 25% of the time. So every fourth customer that lands on that listing will be buying your item just by hitting add to cart. That doesn't mean you can't make sales if you're not the box seller. Like previously stated, more attentive shoppers will look for sellers using FBA as their fulfillment provider as free shipping may be offered.

Just Rinse and Repeat – Fueling Your Selling Machine

With your shipment or shipments now on the way to Amazon, sales will begin to come in. There is no need to stand by your computer. Everything is now in place and sales are on autopilot. Amazon will fulfill your orders, take customer feedback, process returns, and handle any administrative duties. Any questions or concerns you may have can be directed through your seller account to customer service.

So what should you be doing while those 10 headphones sell on autopilot?

Go back to Step One of the formula – Find Best Selling Inventory with a Profitable Markup!

Head back to the clearance section of your favorite retail stores, local book sales, or scour the Internet for daily deals. I like to refer to this step as Fueling Your Selling Machine. Your selling machine is all setup and in great hands (Amazon's), and now its up to you to pump it full of profitable inventory.

I know this is a lot of information, but not many businesses can be fully explained in such a short length. However, this is why I love this business. Anybody with access to a computer and a few dollars can get started, although it does help to have a smartphone for on the go. We've gone over the benefits of using FBA as an Amazon Seller, but I'd like to highlight the benefits of this business to convince you of it's unlimited potential.

The Benefits & Lifestyle of a Retail Flipper

Risk Free

So you've found a Lego toy selling for $8 at your local Toys R Us and selling on Amazon for $24. Bingo! You've found a 3x markup of a great selling children's toy. You quickly whip out the credit card and buy 10 of them, totaling $80. You sell 2 in the first week, but then Amazon decides to start selling them and offers a better price. Their price is too low to match and you get discouraged because you haven't made all of your money back. We'll here's the risk free benefit which most businesses can't offer.

You process an order removal from your seller account and get the 6 Lego toys that did not sell, sent back to your house for a $2 fee. You then take your original purchase receipt and head to your local Toys R Us where you made the purchase. Because they offer a 90-day return policy, you get fully refunded for 6 items.

So, where in most businesses you would have just taken a loss, you actually profited. You were able to sell 2 Lego toys at a 3x markup and only took a $2 loss on the other 6 items by returning them.

It's a risk free business if you are organized and maintain control of your inventory. Make sure you fully understand the timeframes and policies of all of the stores you choose to purchase from. Be very careful with online purchases, as they sometimes can't be returned after a certain amount of time, or don't allow for in store returns.

Choose Your Schedule

I still work a full time job, which demands full time attention. I am still able to run this business successfully in my free time with FBA doing most of my work. I sometimes miss out on early morning sales, but I am able to accomplish a lot after work and on weekends. You can really create your own schedule once you see what works for you. Not many businesses offer this flexibility.

Choose Your Earnings

The more capital and time you spend in this business, the greater your profit. However, you are not limited by your own capital. I've creatively found ways to get my hands on more capital and inventory. Enlist the help of friends and family. Maybe you have a friend who is willing to buy some products and sell on your account because they don't want to deal with all the logistics (although we've just gone through how easy it can be). I've struck agreements with friends where I will list and sell their products and split the profit 50/50. I never put out a dime for the products, but because I have the sellers account, I am earning free money.

Also, I get creative in terms of sourcing product. Book sales, library sales, and clearance sections offer great products for a fraction of the cost. I recently attended a book sale in Brooklyn where I got over 40 books for less than $50. The total profit I will see from these books is over $400. After selling just 3 books, I will have paid for the cost of all 40 books.

For those with greater organization skills and confidence in their abilities to source profitable inventory, there are numerous solutions for acquiring more capital. Using credit cards properly can propel a part time seller to full time status. If you are able to find those hot selling items, you will make your money back within the same month that your credit card bill is due. I have yet failed to pay my credit card bills on time and in full. I only buy items that I know will turnover quickly, enabling me to pay off creditors as well as pay myself within a calendar month.

Lastly, there are several companies that will lend money to online sellers. The easiest company to work with is Kabbage. They work specifically with small to medium size online sellers. By allowing Kabbage to analyze your online selling channels and revenue, they will give you money to buy more inventory. It is much more flexible than a loan due to their great payback program and you will get approved within 20 minutes. I have taken out several thousand dollars from them and the process was painstakingly easy.

Frequent Flier Miles /Rewards Points

With limited capital, I decided to take out several credit cards for just this business. Because I'm constantly "fueling the selling machine", I've racked up some serious frequent flier miles. I have earned about 5 round trip flights within the continental US just for signing up for these cards and hitting certain milestones, all within the first few months.

Birthday Gifts and Personal Items

Occasionally, I find items too good to pass on that don't sell well on Amazon or I rather keep. By surrounding yourself with crazy deals all day, you end up getting items at a serious discount. While I admit I have bought items that I probably would have never purchased otherwise, I've also ended up with many gifts for friends or for during the holidays. Also, I've been stuck with some items due to a certain return policy or online purchase. I could have recouped most of my money by selling, but rather have accumulated a great collection of gifts and gadgets.

The Ultimate Resource Section for Finding Profitable Inventory

Since 90% of a profitable seller's time is focused on finding profitable inventory, I wanted to make sure I fully elaborated on my sourcing strategy. All of my sourcing tips and locations can be categorized into 3 categories: In Store, Online, and Books.

In Store (70% of my purchases)

Strategy

The majority of my purchases are made in store because this is where arbitrage is most likely to happen. All deal seekers will flock to the same places online, ultimately leading to a price drop for most items. In stores, there is very little transparency for what's on sale. Two different Staples may be selling the same item for two different prices, where as the online price is the same. One store may have overstocked a certain item and must get rid of them before new inventory comes in, leading to a massive clearance blowout. There are so many factors that come in to play.

Ultimately, if you find a great deal at one store, you should call all of the surrounding stores and try to reserve as many as possible. There is no need to look for different deals if you can milk one for all its worth. The downside to stores is the limited inventory. If you find a great deal online, you can just add as many units to your cart as possible, but stores only have so many units. You must be willing to travel to get the deals, but it's usually worth it since nobody else will be getting these same deals.

Where to Go

You will find deals everywhere, but will want to find these deals in locations where other stores may offer have deals. Also, different areas of the country boast different stores. My list is what works for me, but you should look to find those stores that work for you. Here's my list in no particular order, with pros and cons for each:

Staples - is a great store because many different savings methods come into play. They occasionally offer great rebates on top quality brands such as Lenovo, Logitech, and Cannon. They don't have the greatest clearance items or sections, but if you master the loyalty savings program and are constantly on the lookout for rebates, you will find success.

Pros: Many locations, lots of electronic goods and accessories, constant rebates
Cons: Not much on clearance so will often leave empty handed unless you have coupons, rebates, and deals ready to go.

Home Depot - is a major wild card, but I wanted to include on this list so you understand that deals can be found anywhere. Most products will NOT sell well on Amazon, but several categories can be very strong. This includes light bulbs, electric drills and tools, and seasonal items that get severely marked down.

Pros: If you find a great buy, chances are you can buy hundreds of that item at a time or visit a nearby store
Cons: No clearance section, takes forever to navigate, very few items that sell super quick

Target – is one of my favorite stores due to their constant clearance sections and clearance markdowns. They make your job easier by applying their red clearance tags on items or yellow/black caution looking signs. They have a lot of electronics, seasonal items, personal care items and occasional will have coupons and deals.

Pros: Large store, usually find a few winners every visit, they have a generous return policy, and they carry several brands or items that can only be purchased at Target (prices actually go up on Amazon after these items sell out in stores)

Cons: Located sparingly, will have long periods without many markdowns

Kohls - is a great store for finding profitable inventory, but the range of products are limited. Personal care items, electronics, and toys are the most profitable items. You MUST sign up for the Kohls Charge Card in order to maximize savings and you should only shop during Sale Periods. During these sale periods, you will receive 10 dollars in Kohls Cash for every 50 dollars you spend. Kohls Cash is credit towards your next Kohls purchases that must occur during a certain time frame. You can construct massive markups if utilizing all the savings methods at Kohls.

Pros: Massive savings periods, hot selling categories
Cons: Must utilize their charge card so you won't earn skymiles, Kohls cash must be spent within certain dates which restricts their effectiveness

TJ Maxx - is a pretty good store to quickly rummage through for electronics and personal care goods. Depending on your location, you may or may not have a store within reach. I wouldn't recommend seeking this store out if it's too far away, but be ready to always walk out with a few purchases if you do have them nearby.

Pros: Guaranteed good deals, hot selling items
Cons: Very limited quantities make it tough to hit it big, odd locations

Radio Shack - isn't one of my favorites, but I have found the occasional steal or two at Radio Shack. These stores are always empty in terms of customers, and I wouldn't be surprised if more and more deals begin to pop up.

Pros: All electronics, easy to navigate, red tags on clearance items, tons of locations
Cons: Not tons of deals, not a lot of inventory so tough to walk out with a bunch of an item

F.Y.E. - is very similar to Radio Shack, but has more selection. They have a great selection of accessories and have occasional clearance sales. You will most likely never get good deals on DVDs or CDs so save yourself the time. This is mostly true across all stores and online shops.

Pros: All electronics, large selection
Cons: Only found in malls, very hit or miss depending on sales

Toys R Us - This store combined with Target will deliver the best retail flipping results for Toys. They also have a great electronics and video game section that is marked up and down with clearance tags. Each store is different so get to know the layout of the ones in your area.

Pros: All toys, lots of clearance items, can buy a lot of one unit
Cons: Disorganization of items

Online (25% of my purchases)

The rest of my time is spent following up with the aforementioned stores online and a few new additions. I will check Kohls, Toys R Us, Best Buy, and Target as they will have occasional sales periods online that offer products not found in stores. Just be wary that all other deal seekers and retail flippers will be ready to pounce on these deals as well.

If I find a really good deal, I will try to buy out the entire inventory so I am assured that I am the only one getting this product. Other retail stores that I will check online include: Best Buy and Kmart. They rarely offer good deals, but Best Buy's outlet section has some good gems.

Deal Aggregators

Aside from the retail stores, I will check deal aggregator sites that pull deals from all sites for your convenience. The best deal aggregator sites at this point in time are:

Slickdeals.net - A highly visited and updated site that features a very active community. You will get the most current deals and coupons right when they come out. Be sure to check often because the deals go fast since there are so many members. If you happen to find a good deal yourself, go ahead and share because you will increase your account status by posting frequently.

Dealcatcher.com – This is a similar site to Sickdeals, but is easier to scan much more quickly as you can scroll through the most recent deals. There is a lot of overlap with Slickdeals, but you will always find differences on each site.

Fatwallet.com – This is a hybrid deal aggregator site. It has forums, coupon postings, and then also a Cash Back program. The Cash Back program allows you to save a small percentage on your online purchases if you make your purchases by first visiting your Fat Wallet account. They will get a piece of your sale because they send you to the online retailer and then will break off a small piece to you. This adds up over time and you can sometimes get up to 10% Cash Back depending on the store and timing.

Deals of the Day Sites

Deals of the Day sites are very popular these days. They offer huge discounts on consumer goods because they buy directly from manufacturers and do not have brick and mortar stores or middlemen that take a cut. Many sites limit the amount of items you can purchase to ensure that end users are getting the goods and not resellers like us. However, a lot of the deals are so good that you can buy 3 and make a good profit, especially if they are expensive electronic goods.

Just know that a lot of people flock to these sites to resell as well and a lot of competition will pop up on Amazon in the coming weeks for those products featured on these sites. If you have the capital to maintain your prices and avoid competing on price, you can make a lot of money from these sites. Here are a few of the sites I've purchased from (be wary of less reputable sites)

Woot – This is arguably the oldest of these sites and has seen great changes. Amazon loosely acquired this site, but has been pretty hands off. You will find a lot of good deals on consumer goods and personal care products. They are slowly raising prices because they have such a following, so deals will be less tempting moving forward.

1SaleADay.com – This site built a monstrous following because they offered the lowest prices on goods for several months after their inception. They often have great deals on electronics, but be careful to read the description. A lot of the deals that sound amazing will feature refurbished goods, so just be sure that it says the product listed is New.

NoMoreRack.com - This site is growing in popularity, but has some reputation problems due to their customer service. They have since cleaned up their act after receiving funding from investors. Keep an eye on this site as they will be offering great deals to try and build up their following.

DailySteals.com – is very similar to 1saleaday.com in terms of types of products they carry. They are very hit or miss, but always worth stopping by to see what the day's deals are.

Coupon Codes

Lastly, before making any purchase online, I check to see if there are any online coupon codes available for my order that will discount the price even further or offer free shipping. I rarely ever pay for shipping and usually get at least another 5% off my purchase with a coupon code. You can find these codes on Retailmenot.com or just by simply Googling "Store Name Coupon Code".

Books (5% of my purchases)

While books don't make up a big portion of my purchases, their revenue sometimes accounts for a lot more. I just want to make it clear that while reselling books can be very profitable, it's very time consuming and competitive. If you find a hot selling electronic item at Target, odds are you can buy 20 of them. If you find a hot selling book at a book sale, that's the only copy you are getting. Also important to note, your time spent on the administrative activities will consume a larger part of your time because you will have to list each individual book, rather than listing just one item where you mark quantity as 20.

On the bright side, books continue to offer the best markups (5-100x). I've found books at book sales for $0.50 that have gone on to sell for over $100 on Amazon. It's an amazing feeling to spend such little money and have Amazon deposit a fat direct deposit into your account.

Since I am not a book-selling expert, I will recommend some resources to help you if you decide you'd like to try selling books.

Finding Books

BookSaleFinder.com – This is the most comprehensive website and directory of all book sales in the country. Any book sale worth attending will be found on this site. If you attend any of these sales, odds are that many other booksellers will be there too.

Library Sales – Call up all local libraries as most of them hold there own sales. These are great for getting cheap inventory without crowds of other booksellers because they are smaller and not advertised. I would suggest making an excel sheet and calling all libraries within a 2 hour radius. They often have a sale every season or even more frequently.

Get Creative – Check your local Goodwill, tag sales, yard sales, and even used book stores. Also, you can make a lot of money selling textbooks. There are various ways to get your hands on textbooks near college campuses.

If selling books seems to grab your attention, I would suggest reading **The Home-Based Bookstore: Start Your Own Business Selling Used Books on Amazon, eBay or Your Own Web Site** by Steve Weber.

The Toolbox of a Successful Amazon Seller

There are very few prerequisites in becoming a successful Retail Flipper, but it helps to be fully equipped with some very useful tools. Below you will find resources that will help at each stage of the retail flipping process.

Getting Started

Amazon Seller's Account – Here you will sign up for your Amazon Seller's Account. (http://services.amazon.com/content/sell-on-amazon.htm/)

Fulfillment by Amazon – Learn more about the FBA services; you can enroll in their service once you've made your seller account. (http://services.amazon.com/fulfillment-by-amazon/benefits.htm)

Step One: Finding Profitable Inventory

Smart Phone – This is pretty much a requirement for all sellers looking to maximize their efficiency for in store purchases. The smartphone allows you to download the Price Check App to get real time pricing and reviews on potential inventory.

Price Check App by Amazon – This free app is available across all smartphones. It allows you to scan the barcodes of items to see what their prices on Amazon are. You can see all sellers and their prices, and sort them by whether or not they are using FBA. You can also see the Amazon Sales Rank, Reviews, and Competition.

Available for Android and iOS

FBA Calculator – Use this calculator provided by Amazon to see how much money you will actually clear for each sale of a product. (https://sellercentral.amazon.com/gp/fba/revenue-calculator/index.html)

For Books - You will probably need to invest in a separate handheld device that is solely devoted to scanning books fast and accurately. The Price Check App is not quick enough to compete with other booksellers rummaging away at these Book Sales, nor will it give extensive information. If you are casually going to buy books like me, you will be fine with just the App.

Transportation – To get full access to arbitrage opportunities, you will want to have a way of getting around. I use a combination of a friend's car and public transportation (I am in NYC so I can get around quickly). Scheduling your trips at the beginning of the month helps you prepare your transportation needs, assemble your coupons for sales, and plan out the routes you will take.

Accessing Capital

Kabbage.com is an online provider of working capital to small businesses. Kabbage can provide you with capital within minutes of signing up.

The Capital One Venture Card (http://www.capitalone.com/credit-cards/venture-rewards) gives me 2x the points for my purchases. They can be redeemed to pay for any travel related purchases on your monthly statement.

Step Two: Leveraging the Amazon Marketplace

Laptop/PC – Another must, but you do not need an incredible expensive machine to get the job done. All you really need a decent Internet connection to log in to your seller account and upload your new inventory.

Laser Printer – A basic label printer will do the trick. I bought a $60 laser printer from Staples and it hasn't let me down. You will just be printing packing slips and shipping labels. You can print the packing slips on regular printing paper, and I would recommend printing the shipping labels on the free UPS label paper.

Label Printer – If you are going to be labeling all of your items, it makes sense to buy a separate label printer such as the Brother Twin Turbo 450 Label printer. Label printers do not use ink or toner, but rather a heating device so you never have to spend money on new ink cartridges. They print incredibly fast, and you can easily peel and place the labels on your items.

UPS Shipping Labels (50 Pack) – These labels can be shipped directly to your door in one day's time. You can order them by making a UPS account online (http://www.ups.com/content/us/en/resources/start/account.html) and heading to the "order supplies" section. Your local UPS delivery guy will drop them off the following day.

Boxes – You can get creative with finding boxes to use for shipping, but I suggest just getting your own large boxes from Home Depot. They cost around $1.50, but you won't find much cheaper anywhere else.

Tape – Shipping tape should be bought in large quantities from your largest retail or wholesale store in the area. It gets very expensive just buying one roll of tape at a time.

Step Three: Rinse and Repeat

You will just need boxes, labels, tape, paper, labels, and an occasional toner cartridge at varying times depending on much volume you are doing.

GrassRootBooks.com Publishing

GrassRootBooks.com is a boutique publishing firm that specializes in publishing fiction and non-fiction Books. We have a number of high-quality works currently available on the Amazon Kindle Store.

Join our newsletter for updates on our latest books, free book promotions, and upcoming releases.

www.grassrootbooks.com/newsletter

At GrassRoot Books, we work with both accomplished and up and coming authors, partnering with talent and producing high quality works. Check out our work at
www.grassrootbooks.com

Printed in Great Britain
by Amazon.co.uk, Ltd.,
Marston Gate.